This Journ

_____

_____

_____

© 2019 Inigo Creations

All rights reserved.
No portion of this book may be reproduced in any form
without permission from the publisher,
except as permitted by U.S. copyright law.

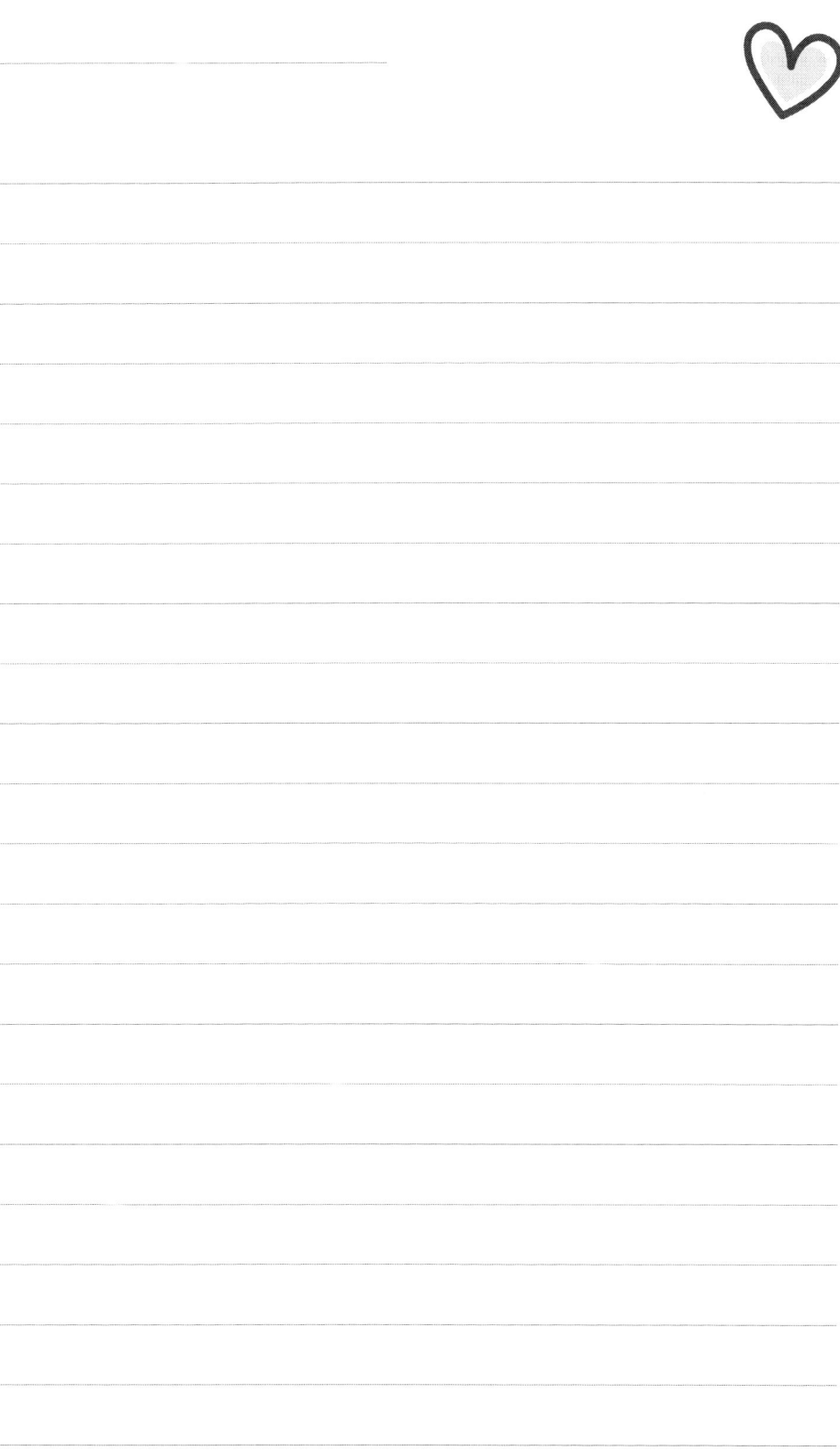

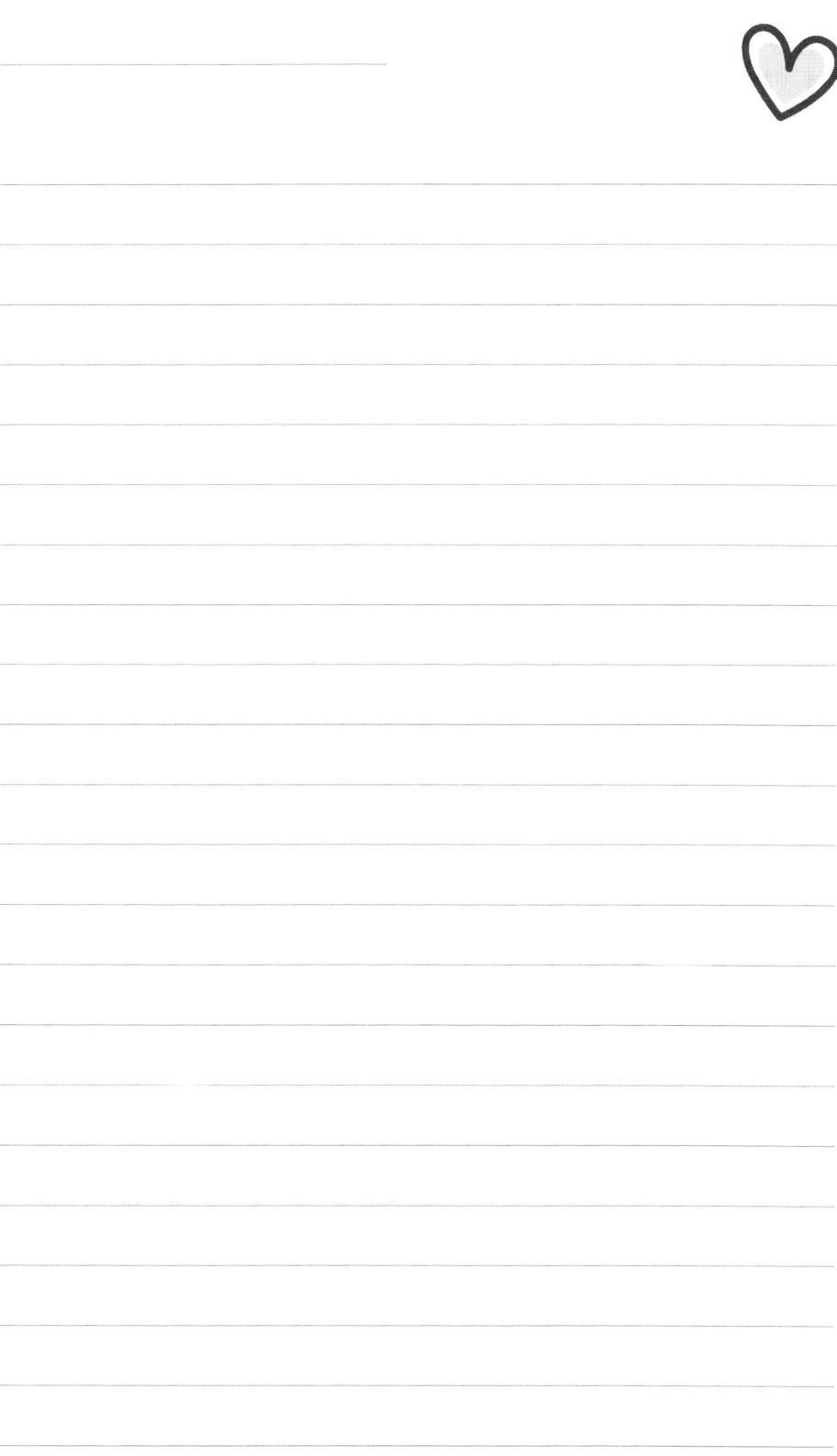

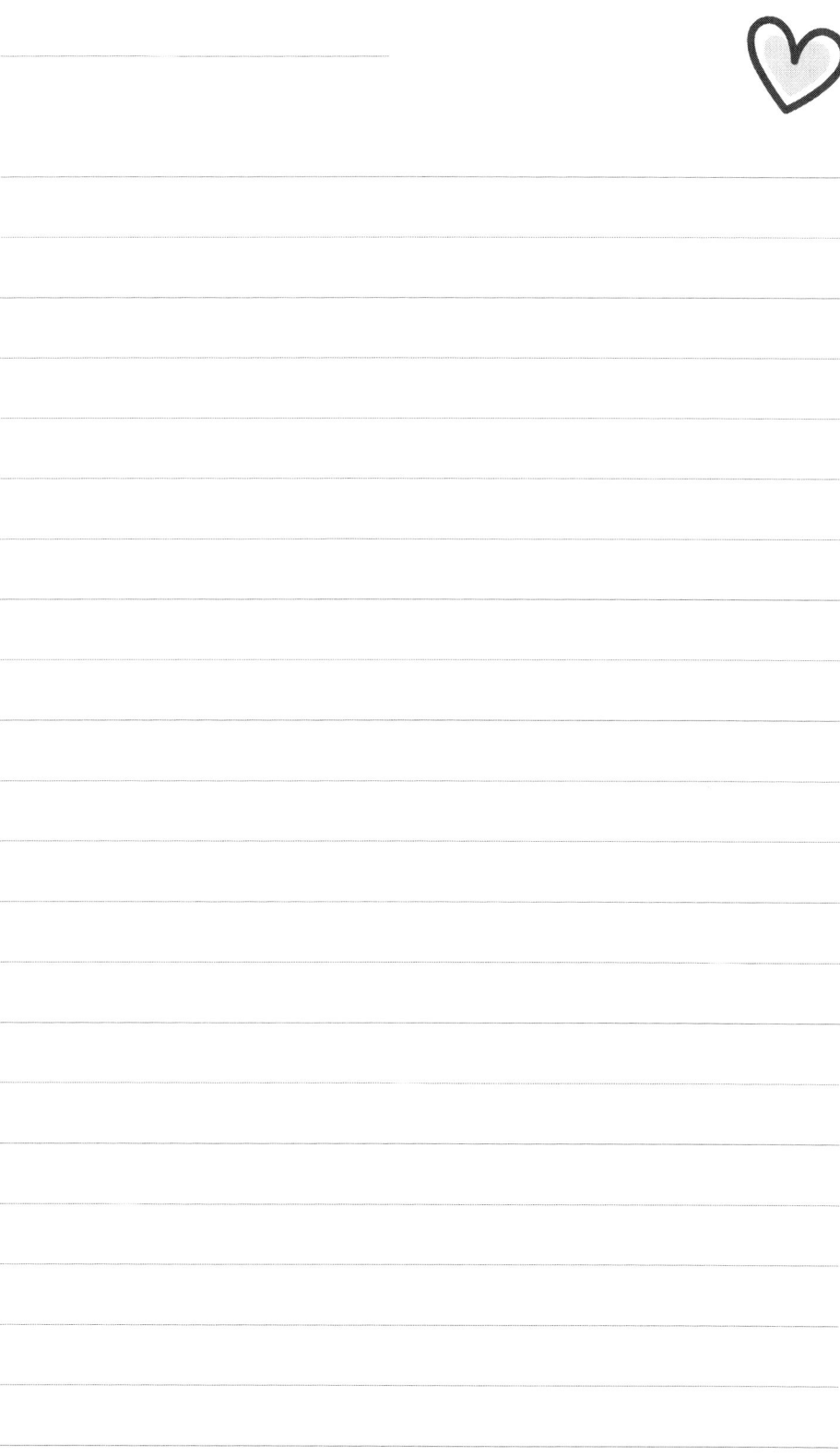

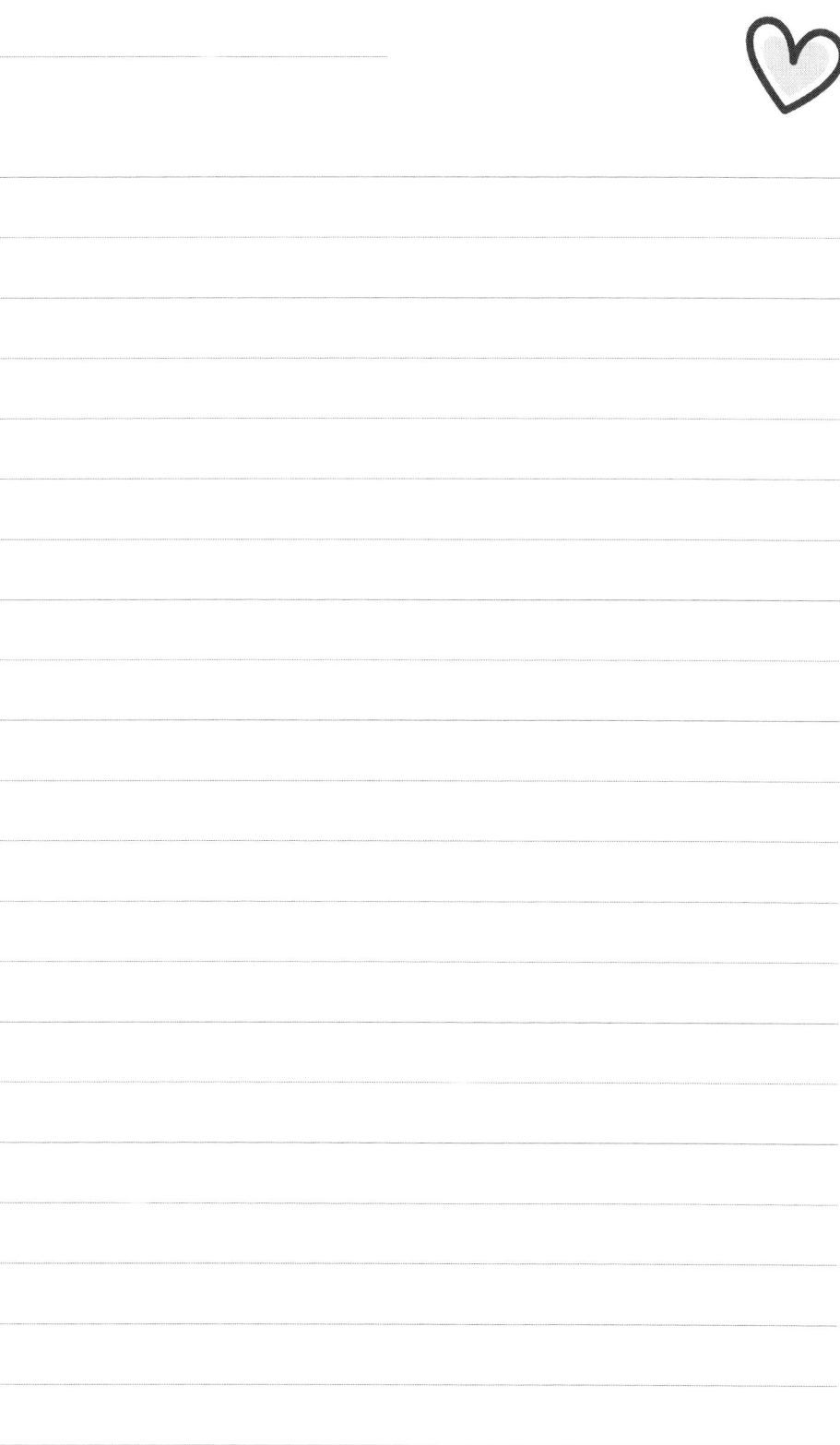

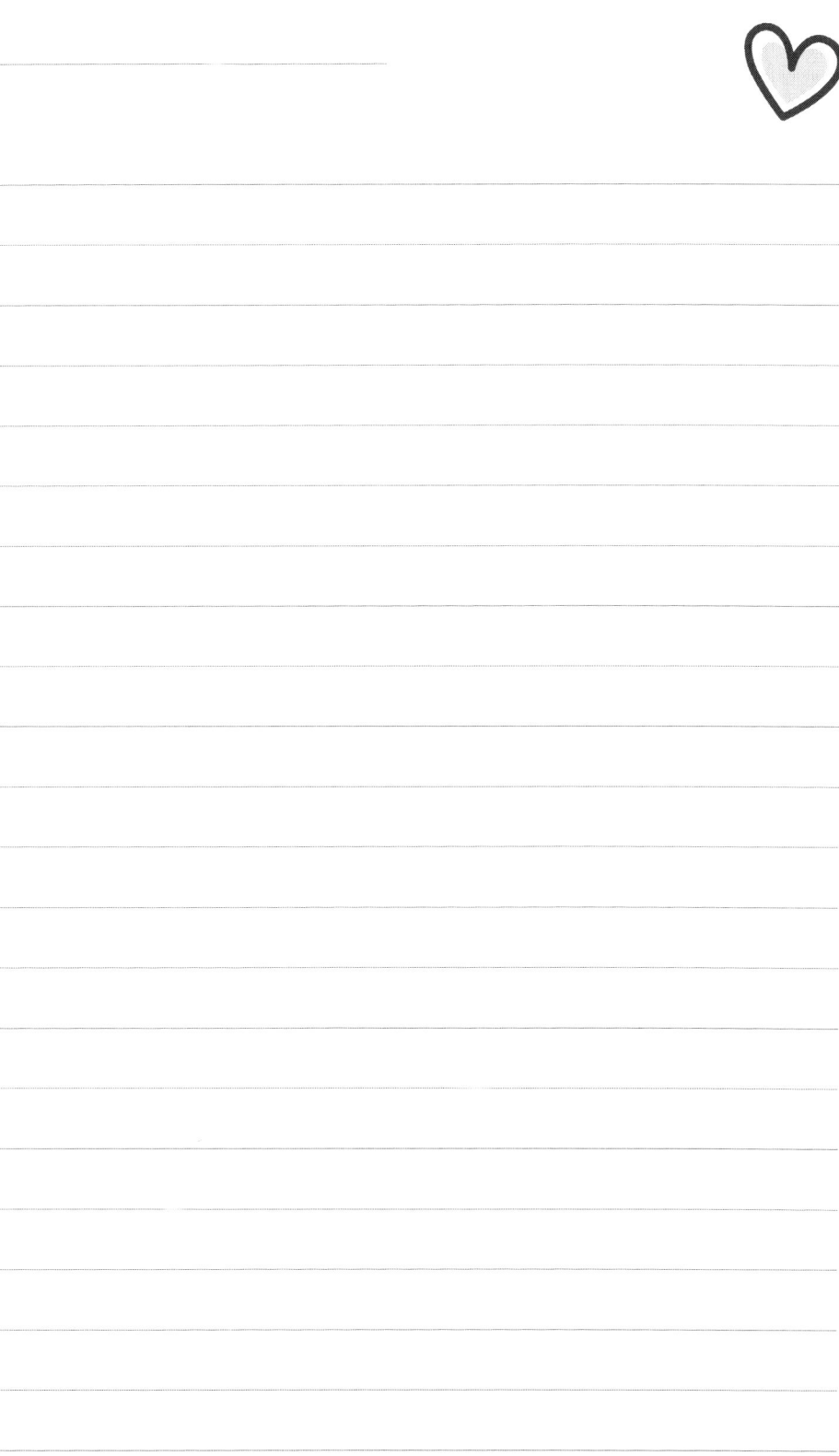

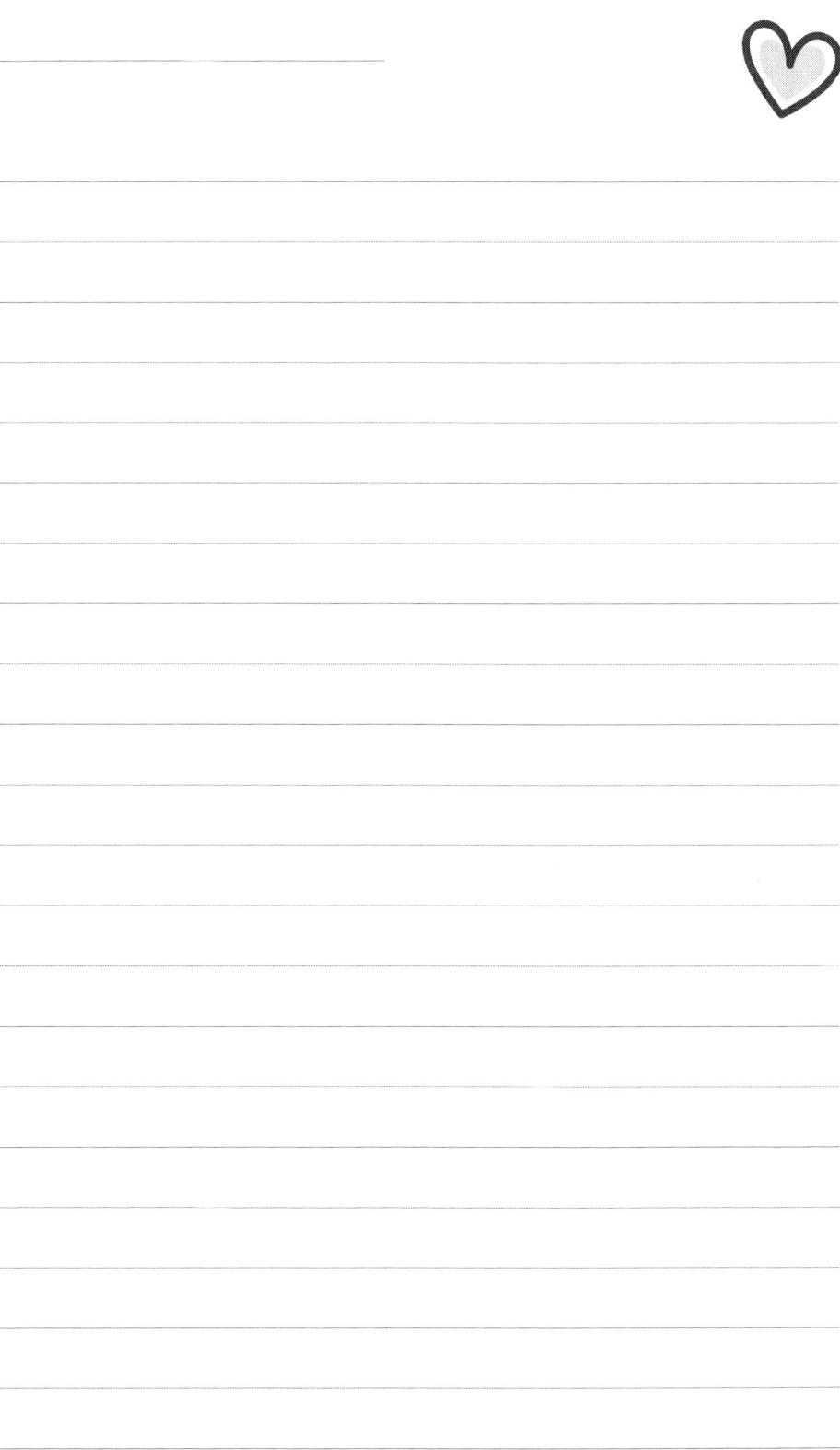

Made in the USA
San Bernardino, CA
18 April 2020